Ichabod Norton, Robert O. Bascom of Fort Edward

Orderly book of Capt. Ichabod Norton of Col. Mott's Regiment

Of Connecticut troops destined for the Northern Campaign in 1776

Ichabod Norton, Robert O. Bascom of Fort Edward

Orderly book of Capt. Ichabod Norton of Col. Mott's Regiment
Of Connecticut troops destined for the Northern Campaign in 1776

ISBN/EAN: 9783742864987

Manufactured in Europe, USA, Canada, Australia, Japa

Cover: Foto ©ninafisch / pixelio.de

Manufactured and distributed by brebook publishing software
(www.brebook.com)

Ichabod Norton, Robert O. Bascom of Fort Edward

Orderly book of Capt. Ichabod Norton of Col. Mott's Regiment

ORDERLY BOOK

OF

CAPT. ICHABOD NORTON

OF COL. MOTT'S REGIMENT

OF CONNECTICUT TROOPS DESTINED FOR THE
NORTHERN CAMPAIGN

IN 1776

AT SKEENSBOROUGH (NOW WHITEHALL), FORT ANN
AND TICONDEROGA, N. Y., AND AT MOUNT
INDEPENDENCE, VT.

TOGETHER WITH A FAC SIMILE OF CAPTAIN
NORTON'S MAP OF TICONDEROGA AND
MOUNT INDEPENDENCE.

WITH AN INTRODUCTION BY
ROBERT O. BASCOM OF FORT EDWARD, N. Y.

—

PRESS OF
KEATING & BARNARD,
FORT EDWARD, N. Y.
1898.

Introduction.

Captain Ichabod Norton, the second son of Thomas Norton, was born in 1736 and married Ruth Strong, February 21st, 1760; he succeeded to his father's estate about three miles north of the meeting house at Farmington, Conn., where he lived most of his life. Following the period covered by the Orderly Book he was in the service, in 1777, at Peekskill, under Colonel Hooker, and for a number of years he represented Farmington in the State Legislature of Connecticut. His eldest daughter, Elizabeth, married the Rev. William Robinson August 10th, 1790. Their son, Charles, had a son Arthur, the father of Charles Mulford Robinson, now of Rochester, N. Y., the present owner of original manuscript Orderly Book. The book itself is somewhat the worse for time and wear. In the Memoir of Rev. William Robinson it is stated that Captain Norton, by his activity and personal example, exerted great influence upon his fellow townsmen in behalf of the American cause. Captain Norton died October 1st, 1825, at Granby, where he then resided. He was the father of nine children.

In printing the Orderly Book an effort has been made to preserve the original spelling as far as possible. The punctuation is that of the editor, and while it would be too much to hope that no mistakes have been made, nevertheless, great care has been taken in reading the proof sheets and in comparing

1

them with the manuscripts, and the hope is enter-
tained that in most cases the meaning is reasonably
clear, and while the writing is not always that of a
literary man, still there is not a word or a line in the
book to indicate that Captain Norton was other
than an honest, earnest, clear headed patriot, endur-
ing great hardship and undergoing suffering and pri-
vation for the benefit of the great cause which he
served. A great many proper names occur in the
work and of these the spelling is not always uniform
nor does it always conform to the modern method
adopted by the several families whose names are here
found, but there can seldom be little real difficulty in
determining what name is intended. Some few
words have occasionally been supplied by the editor;
wherever this has been done the fact is indicated by
the use of parentheses. The map which accompanies
this pamphlet is a *fac simile* of one in the Orderly
Book, except that the letters and explanations have
been added. The book itself does not contain a word
to indicate what the drawing is designed to represent,
still, to one familiar with the locality, there can be no
doubt that it is a rude cut of Lake Champlain, Ticonderoga, Mount Independence, Ti. Creek and East
Creek, and while it is not mathematically correct,
the situations are shown with great fidelity. The
publishers have thought that it would add to the interest and value of the work if a few words were
added here descriptive of the several localities mentioned in the Orderly Book.

Skenesborough is the present town of Whitehall, N. Y., and is situate at the head of Lake
Champlain. It is now a thriving manufacturing

2

and commercial town; it took its name origi-
nally from Major Philip Skene, who established
the first permanent settlement at that place
in 1761, although the Skenesborough patent
was not issued until March 13th, 1765. Major Skene
was a man of considerable means and of great importance in the day and generation in which he lived.
He built a stone house on what is now Williams
street in the village of Whitehall, which was 30 feet
wide and 40 feet long and two and one-half stories
high. He erected a forge on the west side of Wood
Creek, near his house, and one or two saw mills on
the same stream, which here empties its waters into
Lake Champlain. He possessed considerable fore-
sight and enterprise and developed the iron industry
to some extent in what is now Essex county, N. Y.,
and he also constructed a road from Skenesborough
to what is now the village of Salem, in Washington county. He was a Tory and ardently
attached to the cause of Great Britain during the
Revolution. His property was confiscated by the
American authorities, and he was financially ruined
by the result of the war; but few traces of this early
settlement now remain in Whitehall, even the name
of the settlement having been changed though the
student of history may well question whether anything was gained by changing the name of Skenesborough to that of Whitehall. The camp at Fort
Ann, mentioned in the Orderly Book, was situate in
what is now the town of Fort Ann, and here, prior
to the Revolution, upon what is called Kanes Falls,
Major Skene had constructed a saw mill and a block
house. Fort Ann was about half way between Skenes-

borough and Fort Edward. There was a trail from Fort Ann to South Bay, on Lake Champlain, and another one which led to what is now Glens Falls, in Warren county, N. Y. The first Fort Ann was a stockade fort. Skenesborough, Fort Ann and Fort Edward were places of a great deal of importance in our early history. The water route from New York to Canada was up the Hudson river to Fort Edward and thence across the country to Skenesborough, thence by way of Lake Champlain the way was open to Canada. This route, between Fort Edward and Skenesborough, was known as the "Great Carrying Place" because all the munition of war and the *impedimenta* of an army had here to be carried overland between the two waterways, although the situation of what is now known as Fort Edward Creek, which empties into the Hudson river at Fort Edward, and Wood Creek, which debouches into Lake Champlain at Whitehall, is such that they approach one another within the distance of about one-half mile in the vicinity of what is now called Dunhams Basin, and the Indian's canoe or skiff of the white man could be used upon these two streams by making the single carry of half a mile at Dunhams.

Skenesborough, Fort Ann and Fort Edward, came to have a great military importance in our early history, because of their commanding situation upon the Carrying Place. The route here described has well been called the "Great War Trail of the North." So much has been said and written about Fort Ticonderoga that it can hardly be necessary to recount the history of its construction or to enumerate the great and stirring events which there took place and which have served to make it so justly renowned in our history. It stood upon Lake Champlain at the mouth of Ti. Creek, the outlet of Lake George, and was supposed to command the entrance to another water route to the Hudson river from Lake Champlain, the way being up Ti. Creek to Lake George, then through that lake to what is now Caldwell, and thence by a military road to Fort Edward, where the way was again open to New York. Directly opposite Fort Ticonderoga, on the Vermont side, in what is now the town of Orwell, is Mount Independence, and though the name of this place is generally mentioned in connection with that of Ticonderoga, it is not, by any means, so well known to the general public. It is called a Mount by what is in reality a kind of a figure of speech, for it is in truth, but little more than a promontory projecting into Lake Champlain. North of Mount Independence is East Creek, a sluggish stream which takes its rise in the Benson hill east of Lake Champlain and pursuing a northerly and westerly course through the town of Orwell, unites its waters with those of Lake Champlain in a broad, reedy bay which projects into the Vermont shore. East Creek, while it is quite unknown to fame, is not entirely unknown to those who love the sport of trolling for pickerel or hunting for wild duck, and perhaps it has some claim to classic glory through the writings of the Hon. Lucius E. Chittenden of New York, who has perpetuated its memory in sundry pleasing sketches of adventure, the scenes of which are laid upon its placid waters. In the summer and fall East Creek sinks down between its clay banks until its open channel is at places not more than 10 or 20 feet in width, with broad marshes covered with wild oats and bulrushes. These marshes are the feeding ground of large flocks of wild ducks, as they are also the home

5

of the pickerel, and the fisherman, as he pursues his
way up or down the creek, will not unfrequently
arouse the blue heron from its haunts in the marshes.
A little further to the north, on the Vermont side,
is Larrabees Point, in the town of Shoreham. The
Lake Champlain steamers still stop here and it is quite
favorably known as a summer resort and is justly
famed for its beautiful scenery and gorgeous sunsets.
Half a mile north of Larrabees Point is "Hand's
Cove," projecting into the Vermont shore. It was
from "Hand's Cove" that Ethan Allen and his Green
Mountain Boys embarked on that memorable occa-
sion when Ticonderoga capitulated in response to
Ethan's demand made in the "Name of the Great Je-
hovah and the Continental Congress." A little
south of Hand's Cove, on the New York shore. is
Willow Point, where Allen's band of Green Mountain Boys landed. Their course toward the Fort
was along the edge of the lake, passing not far from
where is now situate that unique railroad station
labelled "Addison Junction," on one side and "Ticonderoga," on the other. South of the ruins of the old
fort is Ti. Creek and south of that is Mount Defi-
ance, which commands not only Ticonderoga but
Lake Champlain at this point. There was at
one time a bridge between Ticonderoga and Mount
Independence. "It was a floating structure stretch-
ing over between them and was protected by a boom
thrown across the lake below; above large cassions
were sunk to obstruct navigation." Within the
memory of people yet living traces of this bridge
were yet to be seen. At present a railroad draw
bridge crosses Lake Champlain between Larrabees
Point and Addison Junction. Mount Independence,
in the time when the Orderly Book was written, was
regarded as a place of military importance, and the
ruins which are yet to be seen there richly repay
the tourist for the time and trouble necessary to
visit them. Near the water edge the earthworks
that constituted the "water battery," still five or

6

six feet in height, may yet plainly be seen, and further up the hill, back from the lake, is the "horseshoe battery," so called because of its shape, and though it is now overgrown with cedar and cypress its outline may yet be distinctly traced throughout its whole course, and there may also be found the nameless and unmarked graves of the patriotic dead that here perished during the long struggle between the revolting colonies and the mother country. In 1776 there was a garrison of over 3,000 men at Mount Independence; there was one regiment from each of the States of Pennsylvania, New Jersey, Connecticut, Massachusetts, and several from New York. In the spring of 1776 the camp fever prevailed here to such an extent that from ten to fifteen deaths occurred each day; it began to abate, however, early in September, and had almost entirely ceased by the middle of that month. There was a hospital on Mount Independence, and the ploughshare of the husbandman, not unfrequently to this day, uncovers sundry evidence of the time when the Mount was peopled by a warlike force. In the Orderly Book, under date of October 14th, is a reference to the naval engagement on Lake Champlain between the Americans, under General Arnold, and the British at Plattsburgh. It appears by a letter from Arnold to General Washington, dated October 12th, 1776, that in this engagement there were sixty killed and wounded and that on consulting with General Waterbury and Colonel Wigglesworth it was thought prudent to return to Crown Point. General Philip Schuyler, writing from Saratoga on October 16th, says: "By letters from General Gates and Arnold I am advised of the total destruction of our fleet on Lake Champlain and that it is beyond doubt that the enemy mean to attack our army at Ticonderoga." Something of this expectation of an attack will be noticed in Captain Norton's book during this period. It may interest the reader to know that Mount Independence and the old fort grounds at Ticonderoga have been favorite resorts for the hunter after buried treasure, and the grounds have all been dug over in different places by those who were in search of British gold. Romantic stories are told of these adventures, and by some Ti. Creek has been considered to be the depository of the British treasure chests, and those who are learned in the lore of witch-hazel and divining rods have searched its waters with much care and industry, and it is said that the treasure has often time been located only to be lost by the ill timed exclamation of some enthusiastic searcher; for it is a well known maxim in the art of treasure hunting that the sound of the human voice will instantly cause the treasure to disappear, especially where it has been buried by the use of magic rites, although, of course, we all know that this rule does not apply where gold, silver or any other metal, has just simply been buried without the aid of supernatural agencies. The limitations of this introduction are such as to forbid a detailed account of these numerous attempts to locate the hiding place of the hidden treasure chests, but the mouth of Ti. Creek and the woods near the old French lines on the Fort grounds at Ticonderoga and the vicinity of "Copperas" Rock, on Mount Independence, are the especial localities where this entertaining amusement of searching for hidden treasure has been most industriously carried on in the past. The authorities consulted in the preparation of this introduction are: Bloodgood's Sexigenary, Bottum's History of Orwell, Goodhue's History of Shoreham, Watson's History of Essex County, Chittenden's Capture of Ticonderoga, Fitch's History of Washington County, Journal of the New York Provincial Congress, and Anburey's Travels. I desire here to acknowledge my indebtedness to Dr. D. S. Kellogg of Plattsburgh, N. Y., and to Charles Mulford Robinson of Rochester, N. Y., for information furnished in preparing this introduction.

Fort Edward, N. Y., March 1, 1898.

ROBERT O. BASCOM.

Capt. Ichabod Norton's Orderly Book.

By Samuel Mott, Esq., Col. of a Regiment of Connecticut Troops Destined for the Northern Department, to Capt. Ichabod Norton of Said Regt.

You are hereby ordered to prosed with all Convenant speed to the town of Benington, taking under his command Two Subbalterns and all the men of your compiny who are ready equiped for service; you will prosed by the most convinant way to said town; you will be careful that you march the men as much posible in the cool of the days, lie by in the more sultry hours of and take every other methard to proserve the health of yr men; you will take care that the men Behave Decently & Orderly as you prosed & that they have no disputes amongst themselves or abuse the Inhabitents on the way. Tis expected that you profoorm a march of 20 miles per day and and that there be no unneccasary firing of guns by the men as they pass; itt is supposed every man will be willing to provide himself with 4, 5 or more balls suited to the bore of his gun for any emergency on their march—upon which they will be furnished by Col. Wm. Pitkin at Hartford with one pound of powder to every 8 men, for which you will apply & give your Recept agreeable to an order of the Govt &

Counsel of safety. The men must make up the powder and ball into cartridges and keep itt safe to use against an enemy in case of need; you will use your utmost Vigilence & eare as you pass the upper towns to keep the men from going near to any houses Infected with the small pox & use every method in your power To preserve them from that Disorder. One officer of your Comp., who will be most likely to Inlist men, will remain behind to recrute men for filling up your company & on the 2d Monday of August, with all your men ye shall then have, he will proceed to joyn the Regt. unless he received other orders from me or from his honour, the Gov. On your arrival att Benington you will apply to the commisary there for provisions for the men & you will remain there under the command of the senior officer of sd Regt. untill you have Further orders from me or some other field officer of the Regt. or from His honour, the Govr., or the genll. Given under my hand att Preston, the 26th day of July, ad 1776.

SAMUEL MOTT,
Col. of Said Regt.

———— ———— —— ———

Headquarters, Skeensborough, Augt the 13, Ad 1776.

Officer of the day is Leut. Col. Starr, parowl, heath; Countersign, word; the guard To Consist of 27 Rank and file; the party for fatigue to consist of 3 Subs., 4 Serj., 6 corp. & 170 Rank and file; 1 corp & 3 for guard and 9 for fatigue.

Headquarters, Skeensborough, Augt 14, Ad 1776.

Perowl, word; countersign, heath; field officer of

the day tomorrow is Col. Swift. The guards, the west side the Crick, to be Augmented to 1 Sub., 1 Serj., 1 Corp. and 27 R. and file. The guard on the East Side, as usial; the Party for fatigue to consist of 3 Subs., 4 Serjs., 6 Corp., 170 Rank & file; for fatigue, 1 Serj. 6 privates; 3 For guard.

Skeensborough, Augt 15, Ad 1776.

Porowl, Spencer; Countersign, Putnam; field officer of the day tomorrow is Leut. Col. Starr; Capt. Hooker, officer of the works; the guard, as usial; the party for fatigue tomorrow to consist of 2 Subs., 4 Serjs., 100 Privates; 1 Serj, 1 Corp, 9 privates for Fatigue; Leut Beecher, and 4 for guard.

Headquarters Skeensborough, Augt 16, Ad 1776.

Field officer of the day tomorrow is Major Sumner, Countersign, Spencer; Porowl, Putnam; Capt. Norton, officer of the Works; the guard, as usial; the party for fatigue to consist of 3 Subs, 4 Serjs., 4 Corp. and 150 Rank & file. A weekly return to be made out tomorrow by ten o'clock. It is likewise desired that the commanding officers of Regts see that the quartermasters see that the Vaults are dug that the camp may be kept clean.

DAVID WATERBURY,

Major General.

For fatigue, 13 men, & 2 for guard.

Headquarters Skeensborough, Augt 17, Ad 1776,

Porowl, misfield; countersign, herd; field officer of the day tomorrow is Col. Swift; officer of the works, Capt. Rowley; the guard, as usial; the party for fatigue, the same as this day.   Out of Capt. Nortons Comp., 6 men for fatigue & 1 Corp. and 2 for guard.

Skeensborough Camp, Augt 18, Ad 1776.

Porowl, herd; Countersign, Miflen; field officer of the day tomorrow is Leut. Col. Cortland; officer of the works, Capt. Roboson; the guard, as usual; the party for fatigue is same as this day; 1 Corp., 5 men for fatigue; for guard, 3.

Skeensborough, Aug 19, Ad 1776.

Porowl, Cambridge; Countersign, Roxbery; field officer of the day tomorrow is Leut. Col. Starr; officer of the works, Leut. Wilden; the guards to consist of 1 Sub., 2 Serjs., 2 Corp. and 40 Privates; the party for fatigue the same as this day. It is my desire that if officer or Solgier should know of any infected person of the Small pox, on this ground, and offer to Prove, would give me * * * intelegence. For fatigue, 7 men; for guard, 1 Serj. and 3 Privates.

Skeensborough, Augt the 20, Ad 1776.

Regimental orders, that the Revd. Solomon Morgin is Chaplin of the Regt., and to be obayed as sueh. Charles Mical is Appointed Agitant of the Regt. and obayed as such. asa tracy is appointed quartermaster and is to be obayed as such.   Doct. Apelton Woolcutt Rosseter is Surgeon and Physition to the Regt. and to be obayed as such. Doct. Aron Eliot, Surgeon and Physition mate to the Regt., and to be obayed as such; Jonathan Damands is armour to the Regt. and to be employed and obayed as such. Richard Abby of Capt. Elderkins Comp., is Ap-

12

pointed Ser. Major to the Regt., and to be obayed as such. Ichabod Ward, of Capt. Boolding Comp., is appointed Fife Major and to be obbayed as Such. The Regt is to Attend in the front of the Regt Every Morning and at Evinin the front of Col. Swift's Regt till Further orders. Eight men to attend on Peleg Heart this day, who is to see that Sutible holds be made this day in Sutible Places in the Rear of the Regt. After They are Erected no man is to be found doing his occation in any other place than them aloted, on Penelty of being Confined for breach of orders; the parade to be cleared and Lines Marked out under the Derection of the Agitant. The officers of duty in Each Compiny are to take it by turn day by day and see that the Mens Cooking is well takin care of so far as can be for so small a number of Cittles as can be Contained; the Ravilee to beat in front of the Regt. All Orders, General and Regemental, are to be shone to their officers as Soon as Taken, and Red att the head of Every Compiny att Rowl Call.

Skeensborough, Augt 21, Ad 1776.

Porowl, milford; Countersign, Heartford; field officer of the day tomorrow Col. Swift; the guard as usuil; the party for the fatigue tomorrow the same as this day. if any Solgiers in either Col. Mott's or Col. Swift's Regts wanted Either by Smiths or Carpenders, the Solgiers has a wright to Engage if he Sees fit to forward the work.

Headquarters, Skeensborough, Augt 21, Ad 1776.

Regimental orders: A provision Return of the sevaral Compinys Shall Be made out and Delivered to Peleg Heart, who shall make a return of the Hool. Until the quartermaster who is Back with the bagage shall arive, the Comisind officer of Each Compiny Shall make out their Rowles for their Respective Compinies as Likewise Rowles for their marching Money and proper bills for Bringing their bagage; That application be made to the deputy quartermaster general, who is att Ticonderoga when (Regt) is Paraded or the Compinies formed by the general assembly, viz: Capt. Stephens, Capt. Harmond, Capt. Norton, Capt. Hooker, Capt. Roboson, Capt. Boolding, Capt. Elderkin, Capt. Sharp, the Compinies (will be) ranked. In case of no dispute the Compinies will not determine. That of the officers will, in proper time, be settled according to former servises and present Comisind.

Twas observed Last Evenin, while prayers were attending, that Noise and Singing was made by people who remained in camp, which attended to dissturb Public worship. Tis ordered for futer that no noise or Singing Shall be made In Camp nither Shall the Sutlers offer to sell anything during the time of Devine Servise, unless in case of pure necessity, judged so by the officers of the Regt. The officers and men of the Regt are wellnoing, for the present necessity has obliged the Col. to ask Leave of the general to be absent from His Regt. for a week or two. Col. Mott assures the Regt. that having the highest Hopes & Expectation from the good conduct and harminy of the Regt and Vigilence and alartness in the Servace, nothing less than the alarming, Broken & distressing Situation of his family & affairs could

14

Have tended Him to left Business. But as soon as he has paid a lettle attention to his Molancly affairs att home to return to them without Delay. In the Mean time, hoped and expected that the Comanding officers in the Col.'s absents will intake all posible care of the Regt. to keep them in good order and Disipline & See justice done them on every ocation. The officers and men will pay all due obedience to him as their commanding officer. Tis expected that the officers will take Diligence Care to cultivate in the Men a spirit of good Agreement and Indevour to teach and form them to that fortitude, Resilution and obedience which is the only means of devine protection and victory in case of an attack from the Enemy. Serj. Young, of Capt. Roboson Comp., at tend the office of regimental clark. If the whole of the Regt. should arrive in the Col. Absents, Leut. Col. Worthington will order ye Reg. A monthly return to be made out specifying Each Comp. fit for duty on comand, where at, sick, dead, deserted, absent on furlough, and soforth, having made out, properly sind by himself and transmited to the poast by himself, to Governer Trumbull.

Skeensborough, Agt the 22, Ad 1776.

Regtl. orders: The Quarterguard to consist of 1 Serj., 1 Corp. and 15 Privates, and to be Releivcd att Eight o'clock in the morning and to take them out of the Saviral Comps by a Proper Detail. Bajamin Gale of Capt. Stephens Comp is appointed Fife Major, and to be obayed as such. Lemuel Grigs of Capt. Roboson Comp is appointed Drum Major of the Regt. and to be obayed as such.

Skeensborough, Augt 22, Ad 1776.

Field officer of the day is Col. Worthington. The party for fatigue Amount to 2 Capts, 3 subs, 6 Serjs, 6 Corp, 200 privates; the guard, as usial. As it is nessessary that no filth about the camp, tis my orders that the quartermaster of the Regt. see that the quartermaster serj. see that the Comp Coliman (column) clear of (off) all filth from the Camp and Likewise ordered that there be three men turned out in each Regt to see the foregoing Delay (detail) is done and make a return to the field officer of the day. Itt is my orders that there be 2 Capt, 4 subs, appointed Every day for the works—better service may be done. Capt. Norton's comp, 7 for fatigue and 3 for guard.

Skeensborough, Augt 23, Ad 1776.

Field officer of the day tomorrow Leut. Col. Courtland; the guard, as usuil. The party for fatigue the same as this day—for fatigue, 12 men; for guard, 1 serj.

Skeensborough, Augt. 24, Ad 1776.

Field officer of the (day) tomorrow Leut. Col. Starr; the guard, as usuil. The party for fatigue tomorrow the same as this day. Tis my Positive orders that no person take any Boate or Boates that is above or below the fawls without leave from the officer of the day.

> DAVID WATERBURY,
> Brigadier General.

1 Serj. and 9 for fatigue & four for guard.

Skeensborough, Augt 25, Ad 1776.

Field officer of the day tomorrow is Col Swift; the day guard as usial. The party for fatigue tomorrow the same as this. The carpenders that engage themselves to work at the ship yard must draw provision with the carpenders, that they may not be hindered on the acount. Likewise, I have herd that there (are) some cattle strayed away. I would have Mr. Taylor call for 10 men and fit them out to go till they look them up, as it is of the greatest importence to save our provision. Ten men for fatigue and 5 for guard.

Skeensborough, Augt 26, Ad 1776.

Field officer of the day tomorrow Leut. Col. Cortland; the guard as usial. The party for fatigue the same as this day. Itts ordered that four men be set apart to attend the buchars to bury the guts and nastiness with Blood of the cattle that is cild and likewise ordered that Buchards take care that no nastiness is hov in the crick. If they Heeve any in they must suffer the consequence. Likewise I would have the buchards take care and order better for the futer, or else I shall take care of them. For guard, Ensin James Hecox, and 5 privates and 10 for guard.

Skeensborough, Augt 27, Ad 1776.

Field officer of the day tomorrow Col. Swift. The party for fatigue tomorrow the same as this day and the guard as usial. For fatigue, 4 men and 5 for guard.

Skeensborough, Augt 28, Ad 1776.

Field officer of the day tomorrow is Leut. Cortland; the guard, as usial. The party for fatigue the same as this day—for fatigue, 10 men; for guard, 5 men.

Skeensborough, Augt 29, Ad 1776.

Field officer of the day tomorrow is Col. Swift; the guard, as usial. The party for fatigue the same as this day—5 men for fatigue and 1 for guard.

Skeensborough, Augt 30, Ad 1776.

Regtl orders: That the officers of each Comp See that their men have their arms in good order and that two men out of each comp to assist the armour in erectin a place for to repair the armes, and for the futer the quarterguard to consist of 1 Serj., 1 Corp. and twelve men for the guard, and set two at a time, night and day. Field officer of the day to-morrow is Leut Col Courtland. The party for fatigue tomorrow the same as this day; the guard, as usial—2 for main guard, 2 for quarter guard and 5 for fatigue.

Skeensborough, (Augt) 30, Ad 1776.

Field officer of the day tomorrow Leut. Col. Starr; the guard, as usial. The party for fatigue the same as this day. It is orderd that each ordayly Serj of each comp make a morning report of the sick to the doctors of each Regt, with names to the Doctors, who is to inspect into the circumstances of Such Sick Solgiers and the doctors is to report to the capt how many he finds sick in His comp, and the Doctors who

18

is to make a return to the company for such hospital stores as the solgiers stand in need of. The comanding officers of each Regt, who is to sign the order that shall be given on the comp, and it's orderd that sick solgiers that draw hospital stores is not to draw their Rasions out of the stores, only such as the Doctors should think they stand in need of. It (is) Likewise ordered that the company will provide all ingrediences for the use of the sick, and that to be delt in proper order. 11 men for guard.

Skeensborough, Sept. the 1, Ad 1776.

Field officer of the day tomorrow Leut. Col. Cortland; the guard, as usial. The party for fatigue to consist of 2 capts, 24 Subs, 6 Serjs, 6 corps, 150 Privates. Acording to former orders, A Sub. to be appoynted by the agitant of each Regt over night, to go round the camp the next day and see that the Solgiers keep themselves clean and have their provision cooked in good order. I shall expect these orders will be punctuably fulfild. Captain Norton, officer of the fatigue party, and 5 men, and 4 for guard.

Skeensborough, Sept. the 2, Ad 1776.

Field officer of the day tomorrow Col. Swift; the guard, as usial; the party for fatigue the same as this day; for fatigue, 5 men and 4 for guard.

Skeensborough, Sept. 3, Ad 1776.

Field officer of the day tomorrow Leut. Col. Starr; the guard as usial; the party for fatigue is as this day. A solgiers coat being found, any person Describing and come and Lay Proper claim to the coat

19

by applying to Leut. Milton, of Capt. Mathews Comp., in Col. Swift Regt., Shall have the same. For fatigue, 5 men; for guard, 1 Corp. and 4 Privates.

Skeensborough, Sept. 4, Ad 1776.

Field officer of the day tomorrow Cap. Boolding; the guard to consist of 2 Serjs., 2 Corps. & 50 privates; the party for fatigue to consist of 2 Subs., 3 Serjs. 3 Corps. and 30 Privates; for fatigue, 1 corp. & 3 privates; for guard, 4 privates; Leut Starr to oversee the mens cookery.

Skeensborough, Sept. the 5, Ad 1776.

Officer of the day tomorrow is Capt. Couch; the guard, as usial; the party for Fatigue is one Sub., 2 Serj., 2 Corp. and 35 Privates; for guard, 4 men & 1 corp.; For fatigue, 3 men.

Skeensborough, Sept. the 6, Ad 1776.

Officer of the day tomorrow Capt. Harmon; the guard, as usial; the party for Fatigue tomorrow the same as this day. A weekly Return to be made out tomorrow By Twelve o'clock.

Skeensborough, Sept. the 8, Ad 1776.

Regtl. orders is that Capt. Stephens, Capt. Harmond, Capt. Roboson, with their Compinies, to embark tomorrow morning on the Battoose, to proseed to ticonderogue and those on duty in either of aforesaid compinies to be Emediately Releevd by the other compinies.

WILLIAM WORTHINGTON,

Leut. Col.

Fortann Camp, Sept. the 11, Ad 1776.

The orders for tomorrow are that a corp. guard be mounted and 1 Serj., 1 corp. and 10 privates turn out on the Working party at half after 7 o'clock. cet 1 corp. and 3 privates for fatigue and 3 for guard.

WORTHY WARTERS,

Major.

Foortann Camp, Sept. the 12, Ad 1776.

The orders for tomorrow are that a guard be mounted as usial; the party for fatigue the same as this day; 1 serj. and 3 privates for guard & 1 Corp. and 3 privites for fatigue.

WORTHY WARTERS,

Major.

Camp att Fortann, Sept. 13, Ad 1776.

The orders for tomorrow are that A corp. guard be mounted as usial and 1 serj., 1 corp. and 10 Privates turn on the working party.

WORTHY WARTERS,

Major.

For guard, 3 men; For fatigue, 1 corp. & 2 privates.

Fortann Camp, Sept. 14, Ad 1776.

The orders for tomorrow are that Corp. guard be mounted as usial and 1 Corp. & 10 privates turn out on the Working party.

WORTHY WARTERS,

Major.

1 corp. and 3 Men for guard and 2 for fatigue.

Fortann Camp, Sept. the 15, Ad 1776.

The orders for tomorrow are that a corp. guard be mounted as usial and that 1 corp. and 10 privates turn out on the working party.

WORTHY WARTERS,

Major.

Fortann Camp, Sept. 15, Ad 1776,

The orders of this day is that 1 Sub. of Capt. Nortons Comp. march from this camp four miles, to a dwelling house, with 15 privates, and there to remain till further orders, with 6 days provision, to work on the roads.

WORTHY WARTERS.

Major.

Fortann Camp, Sept. the 16, Ad, 1776.

The orders for tomorrow are that A Corp. guard be mounted as usial and corp. and 10 privates turn out on the working party.

WORTHY WARTERS,

Major.

3 men for guard & 1 corp. for fatigue.

Camp att fortann, Sept. the 17 Ad 1776.

The orders for tomorrow is that A Corp. guard be mounted as usial and 2 men go to help down with sheep, to Skeensborough, and 2 men to work at the sawmill, and 2 men to keep sheep here, and 1 corp. and 6 privates turn out on the working party. 1 corp. and 3 privates for guard and 2 for fatigue.

Camp att Fortann, Sept. the 18, Ad 1776.

The orders for tomorrow are that a corp. guard be mounted as usial and 1 corp. and 10 privates turn out on the working party.

WORTHY WARTERS,
Major.

For guard, 3 men, and 1 for fatigue.

Camp att Fortann, Sept. the 19, Ad 1776.

The orders for tomorrow are that a corp. guard be mounted as usial and a corp. and 9 privates turn out on the working party.

WORTHY WARTERS,
Major.

1 corp. and 2 privates for guard, and 1 man to keep sheep.

Camp att fortann, Sept. the 20, Ad 1776.

The orders for tomorrow are that a corp. guard be mounted as usial and 1 corp. and 9 privates turn out on the working party at 8 o'clock, and the orderly serjs. see that them men Parade Exactly by the time. for the futer all firing is strictly forbid, and any person who shall fire his gun in the camp without leave from Capt. or his Commanding officer, may expect to suffer for it as breach of orders.

WORTHY WARTERS,
major.

Camp att Fortann, Sept. the 21, Ad 1776.

The orders for Tomorrow are that a corp. guard be mounted as usial & 1 Subs, one corp. and 22 privates turn out on the working party for one week, and take 7 days (rations) with them and to parade tomorrow morning at 8 o'clock.

WORTHY WARTERS,

Major.

For guard, 1 corp. and 3 privates, and 1 Serj. and 8 privates for fatigue.

·

Camp att Fortann, Sept. ye 22, Ad 1776.

The orders for tomorrow is that a corp. guard be mounted as usial and 3 men to go on fatigue and all who are A mind to draw molases may draw tomorrow one week alowance for man.

WORTHY WARTERS,

Major.

For guard, 3 men; 1 for fatigue.

Camp att fortann, Sept. ye, 22, Ad 1776.

The orders for tomorrow is that a Corp. guard be mounted as usial and 3 men to go on fatigue.

WORTHY WARTERS,

Major.

For guard, 1 Corp. and 3 privates, and 1 man for fatigue.

Camp att fortann, Sept. ye 24, Ad 1776.

The orders for tomorrow are that corp. guard be mounted as usial and three men to go on fatigue.

WORTHY WARTERS,

Major.

3 men for guard, 1 for fatigue.

Capt. Norton's Orderly Book.

- - - - - - - -

Were any of Your Ancestors in the Revolutionary War?

If so, you ought to own this Book.

- - - - - - - -

We have recently come into possession of a valuable, old and original manuscript. It is Captain Ichabod Norton's Orderly Book, of the war of 1776. Although the book is somewhat the worse for wear and age, we have, in publishing it, endeavored to preserve the original spelling and phraseology as nearly as possible, believing that it will be sought for by historians and all interested in revolutionary times, especially those whose ancestors, hailing from Connecticut, Pennsylvania, New Jersey and New York, took part in the war of 1776. It was written in 1776 at Fort Ann, Skenesborough (now Whitehall), Ticonderoga, New York and at Mount Independence in Orwell, Vermont. Captain Norton belonged to Col. Mott's Regiment, from Connecticut, in the "Northern Department." It commences with the beginning of the campaign, in July, 1776, and ends November 25th of that year, and contains almost daily entries during this period. Connecticut had two regiments at Ticonderoga in this campaign viz: Mott's and Swift's. The officers were as follows:

Brig. Gen., David Waterbury of Stamford.
Col., Samuel Mott, Preston.
Lieut. Col., William Worthington, Saybrooke.
Major. John Sumner, Middletown.
Paymaster, Timothy Larrabee.
Capt. First Co., Aaron Stevens, Kellingworth.
Capt. Second Co., John Harmon, Jr., Suffield.
Capt. Third Co., Ichabod Norton. Farmington.
Capt. Fourth Co., Ozias Pettibone, Simsbury.
Capt. Fifth Co., Elijah Robinson, Stafford.
Capt. Sixth Co., Josiah Baldwin, Kellingworth.
Capt. Seventh Co., Vine Elderkin, Windham.
Capt. Eighth Co., Elijah Sharp, Windham County.
  Swift's Battalion—Col., Herman Swift, Cornwall; Lieut. Col., Josiah Starr, New Milfred; Maj., Stillworthy Waters; Chaplain, Rev. William Tennent, Greenfie'd.

The publication will also contain a hitherto unpublished map of the locality named, and has an introduction written by R. O. Bascom of Fort Edward, N. Y., containing a description of the localities where the Orderly Book was written. The book abounds in interesting descriptions of the daily proceedings of the army and is uncommonly rich in proper names and affords some information as to almost every one of the persons mentioned. The following extracts are made from the book:

"Skeensborough, August 24th, Ad 1776.
   *   *   Tis my positive orders that no person take any boate or boates that is above or below the fawls without leave from the officer of the day.
                    DAVID WATERBURY, Brigadier General."

"September 3d.
   *   *   A solgiers coat being found, any person Describing and come and lay Proper claim to the coat by applying to Lent. Milton, of Capt. Mathews Comp., in Col. Swift Regt., Shall have the same."

"Camp att fortann, Sept. 17. Ad 1776.

The orders for tomorrow is that A Corp. guard be mounted as usial and 2 men go to help down with sheep to Skeensborough, and 2 men to work at the saw mill, and 2 men to keep sheep here.   *   *   "

"Mount Independent, October ye 9, Ad 1776.

Regt. orders: The armour of the rogt. is to attend strickly to fit up ye arms of the Comps. without delay. To begin att Capt. Hookers comp., then Capt. Norton comp., then Boldings, then Capt. Charp, then Capt. Elderkins   *   *   "

"Mount Independence, October 14, Ad. 1776.

*   *   As the enemy is ourly expected an atack this Camp, it is expected the Regt. under arms every morning att 4 o'clock, and repair with all silence to the alaraming poast and stand there till Broad day light.   *   *   "

"October the 15, 1776.

*   *   Capt. Jones on the Side of ticonderogue and Major Bigelow will resume the comand of Artilary on Mount independent.   *   *   "

"October the 17, Ad 1776.

The comesary is Emediately to isue out half a gill of rum to Every Non comisind officer and soigier now in camp, and should the wet weather hold till evining he is (to) isue one half gill more.   *   *   Mr. Robert Hops is appointed quartermaster of the first Battalion of pennsylvania In the room of Quartermaster Nickels, and John King is appointed Ensign in tho room of Mr. Coy, dead, in the same Battalion of Pennsylvanians.   *   *   "

"Head quorters, November 13th, Ad 1776.

The first Battallion of Pensylvanians and first 2 of the Jersey Regts. are to be taken of (off) duty & prepair to embark for foort George as soon as the Battoas are ready that will be Appointed to carry Them over tho lake.   *   *   "

Beside the Connecticut troops there were regiments from Pennsylvania, New Jersey and New York, stationed at these points, during the period covered by Captain Norton's book and the work abounds in the names of officers from those states and cannot fail to be of great value to all who are interested in the revolutionary record of their ancestors.

Among the many names mentioned are the following:

Aba	Doughton	Maxwell	Sholds
Adams	Downs	McCoy	Sherman
Allen	Drawer	McDaniels	Sliby
Armistead	Dunn	Milton	Smith
Armstrong	Eliot	More	Summers
Arnold	Faset	Morrill	Sumner
Ballard	Field	Morrison	Stark
Baldwin	Frazer	Morris	Stacey
Baker	Fuller	Morgan	St. Clair
Ban	Foote	Mott	Starkweather
Barnet	Gale	Nichols	Starr
Bason	Goodel	Norton	Stephens
Bates	Gordin	Ogden	Swift
Beecher	Graton	Osborn	Taffen
Biglow	Griggs	Patison	Tassett
Bliss	Harmon	Parrett	Trip
Bolding	Harrison	Parker	Trumbull
Bond	Hale	Perry	Twist
Bragg	Harper	Persons	Waterbury
Brayman	Harvey	Pheney	Ward
Brewar	Hammon	Pike	Waters
Brown	Hay	Pitkin	Wayne
Brooks	Heart	Porter	Warner
Buel	Hecox	Pots	Wagmon
Burrel	Hooker	Poor	Walker
Bush	Hope	Powers	Walingford
Butler	Holmes	Pownell	Welch
Byan	Homes	Pratt	Wheelock
Canady	Howland	Randall	Whitcomb
Carter	Howell	Read	Whitmore
Cheney	Hughes	Rice	Whitney
Cilly	Hunting	Richardson	White
Cole	Jackson	Rion	Wilden
Cowell	Johnson	Ripply	Wingate
Couch	Jones	Rogers	Willard
Courtland	King	Robards	Win
Coy	Lenard	Rossoter	Willow
Cragg	Lewis	Robinson	Wigglesworth
Culver	Lyon	Rowley	Washington
Daniels	Lyman	Ryan	Woodbridge
Daton	Matthews	Scott	Wood
Dickinson	Marsh	Senter	Worthington
Dockerday	Marcome	Sharp	Wright
Dole	Marshfield	Sherborn	Young
Doglass	Marquise	Shepherd	

This book is something out of the ordinary and if you are at all interested in historical facts you will find between its covers that which will be of great interest. The edition is limited to 250 copies. It is placed at the low price of $1.00 per copy, and those who desire to obtain one should address,

The Keating & Barnard Publishing Co.

FORT EDWARD, N. Y.

The edition is limited to 250 copies

Camp att fortann, Sept. the 25, Ad 1776.

The orders for tomorrow are that the guard and fatigue the same as this day.

WORTHY WARTERS,
Major.

For guard, 1 corp. and 3 privates; for fatigue, one man.

Camp att fortann, Sept. ye 26, Ad 1776.

The orders for tomorrow are that the guard and fatigue as this day.

WORTHY WARTERS,
Major.

For guard, 3 men; for fatigue, 1 man.

Fortann Camp, Sept. the 27, Ad 1776.

The orders for the day tomorrow are that the guard and fatigue the same as this day.

WORTHY WARTERS,
Major.

For fatigue, 1 man; for guard, 1 corp. and 3 privates.

Camp att fort ann, Sept. ye 28, Ad 1776.

The orders for tomorrow are that a corp. guard be mounted as usial and four men turn out on the fatigue party.

WORTHY WARTERS,
Major.

For guard, 3 men; for fatigue, 2 men.

Camp att fortann, Sept. the 29, Ad 1776.

The guard, as usial; the party for fatigue tomorrow the same as this day.

WORTHY WARTERS,

Major.

Ticonderoguege, Oetober ye 3, Ad 1776.

Regt. orders: Capt. Roboson, with Leut. Aba and 2 serjs. and 54 men, are amedeately to get Rady and to proseed with 6 Battoes, ordered by the general, to Skeensborough, and bring forward a drove of sheep and in the care of Mr. Morgin, Esq., who will Attend in bringing them forward. Capt. Roboson, with his boats and sheep, will make no delay in Bringing to this place. The party will consist of sixteen men of those who has been imployed in getting Cord wood, as many as can be speard from Capt. Sthephens, Harmon, Roboson Compinies, and to be compleated by the other comps. of the Regt. a true and exact return be made tomorrow morning of the state (of) each comp. in the Regt Spacifying the pace (place) and cituation of all the officers and men— every one dead, every sick, every one absant, so that a true return of all the original Nombers of the regt. may be asserted.

Head quarts, ticonderoguege Camp, att mount of Independence, October ye 4, Ad 1776.

In consequence of the wet weather, the comesary is to isue one gal. of Rum to each non comisind officer and solgier in camp. As the general court marshal, of which Major moroson (is) presedent, Stephen

Tuffen, serj. in Col. Whelock Regt, tried for leaving his guard without orders, in the corse of the trial and itt appeared to be more a mistake than Desine, the cort finding him not gilty. James Matsews, of Col. Pores Regt., tryed by the same court marshall for stealing a shirt and conseling; after the court having considered the evidence are of (the) oppinion that The prisinor was not gilty of consealing but from the continuance of the Desposier of ye hanger, after it was claimed by the owner; finding—guilty of conseling; but from the continuance of the desposier of the Hanger, after it was claimed by the owner; finding—guilty of conseling itt, and ordered that he pay ten Shilling Lawfull money To Leut. Moroson, the owner, as A Composition for the hanger. The general Approved the Aforesaid Sentance and ordered them to take place Immediately. The general cort marshal, of which Major morice, president, is Desolvd. The following comosions (promotions) are ordered to take place, Namely : In Col. Woodbredge's Regt., Mr. Samuel Lenward, Quarter master, vice qu. master Duglis, advanced; 2 Leut. Dickinson, first Leut., vice Leut. Bason, dead; Ensn Abner Lyman, 2 Leut., vice Dickingson, advancd; Serj. major, advance Ensn; Ensn Lyman, advancd, 2 leut Powers Dead ; Ensn Caleb Brayman, 2 Leut. vice Leut. Goodel, advancd; Serj. isaac Chuck, Ensn, vice Ensn advanced. In Col. Whitcom Regt.: 1 Leut. Roger Dence, Cap., vice Capt. Harison, dead; 2 Leut. Joshua Fuller, 1 Leut., vice Ensn Solomon Richardson, 2 Leut. Field officer of the day tomorrow, for Ticonderoguege, Col. Wane; Brigade major Brown. field officer of the day tomorrow, for mount

Indepen (Independence), Col. Wairman; Brig. major Rice. The Battoes guard to consist of 1 serj., 1 corp. and 12 men.

Mount Independant, October ye 5, Ad 1776.

General orders. The following comotion are ordered to take place in the Six of Col. Whitcoms Regt.: 1 Leut. thomas Witington, Capt., Vice Cap. Ballard dischargd; 2 Leut. Tocerman, 1 Leut., vice Willington; Ensn Dockerday, 2 Leut., vice Leut. Turarman, promoted; Serj. Dockerday, Ensn, vice Ensn Dockerday, promoted; 1 Leut. Noah Allen. Capt.; Solomon Richards, 2 Leut.; Serj. Maclair, ensn, Ensn Smith promoted. Field officer of the day tomorrow Col. S. Swift; brigad major howel.

Mount Independant, October the 5, Ad 1776.

Regt. orders. Whereas a great many officers and solgiers of the Regt. are sick and many in a dangerous situation, and whereas the exsegence of the servace has caused the Regt. to be much Devided in parts, a consider(able) body att this place and other considerable parts at Skeensborough & another of the like at fortann, and the Fasition of the Regt. & his mate not being able to attend the duty for the comfort of the sick in the Regt., and as Leut. Macclure has for three weeks attended the sick to a very good purpis in the regt., this therefore orderd, that Leut. macclure, of Capt. Roboson's comp., being exscused from duty of A sub. and assist as a Fasition in attending the sick of the Regt. till furder orders.

Camp att Mount independant, October ye 6. Ad 1776.

A general cort marshal, the lines to set tomorrow morning at ten o'clock, in one of the old forts, & for the tryal of Capt. Jonathan and John Foshct and three Leut. belongs of Independant—sartain Non comisind officers and solgiers of the three comp.—the former for leaving his poast without orders or being attack by the enemy; the latter for breaking all orders. All persons concerned to attend the court. The artificers and labourers to the sawmill, for futer, to be under derection and payment of the deputy quarter master general, who is (to) dismiss all who is Negligence of their duty, without delay; to Imploy others in their room. The Comesary is to issue half a gill of rum for man to non comisind officers and solgiers who returned from guard. Every morning at nine o'clock the officers coming of (off) guard to sign the return to the comesary. The former work on mount Independant now completed. The three brigades on the mount, hundred men, in following to proposion, viz: The first brigade, 56 men; 2 brigade, 102 men; 3 brigade, 154 men—two hundred are to be Imployed in cutting pickets; one hundred in diging a trench & Foundation for a magizene for powder. This party to be furnished dayly and to be (under) the derection of Col. Patison and Col. poor. The officers and subs., as they shall be appointed for the cort marshall, orderd above : The brigadear general, president;   Col. poor, Col. Wayne, Col. Erman ogden, Sheror Lenyardhart, majors. Sherborn, Rem, Detrart, Hail and Butler, Capts. ; hamour, the first Penselvanian Battalion; Judge advocate of the court.

Field officer of the day tomorrow, att Ticonderoguege, Col. Whelock; Brigade major Brown. field
officer of the day for Mount independant Col. S.
Mott, Brigade major of the 2 brigade.

*Ticonderoguage, mount independant, Oct. ye 7, Ad
1776.*

Regt. orders: The commanding officers regts. are
Immediately order all the spades and shovls now in
use in their respective comps. to be colleeted forth-
with by the quarter master, such as are on Ticonderogue side of the lake; and the spads and shovls on
mount independent are to be delivered to headquarters Att Col. Patison Regt.   works is equily in
want of their tools. The general desires the commanding officers of regiments will command strict
obidience to these orders. The following comotions
are ordered to take place in Col. Patison regt. : Ensn
David Johnson, 2 Leut., vice Leut. Johnson, dis-
charged; serj. major William Cheney, ensn. Field
officer of the day tomorrow, Leut. Col. Brown;
Brigade major Byan. for mount independant, Leut.
Coovell, brigade major howel.

Ticonderoguege Head quarters, Oct. ye 8, Ad 1776.

Genl. orders: The comesarry is to isue four sheep to
each regt; 3 sheep to corps of artiliry; 3 to the sheep
artficers at the usial time of drawing provision. The
commanding officers will derect the 8 week solgiers
to be suplied with those ingrediences, the comesarys
to recon the sheep in the alowance to the Regts. att
their estimated weight. The pork barrels in the
prosestion (possession) of the respective Regt. are to

30

be emediately colected and delivered by the Quarter
masters to mr. young, for the purpis of Salting beef.
No Person is to apply for a discharge in futer unless
he bring with him to headquarters the Sutificut and
reseet of pay hertafore orderd. A form of each of
these is this day given to each major of brigades and
no dischargd will be given unless the Sutificate coro-
spond with that form. Field officer of the day tomorrow, for Ticonderogue side, Leut. Col. Robards;
brigade major Brown. Field officer of the day tomorrow, for mount independan, Leut. Col. Senter,
brigade major the 2 brigade.

Mount Independant, October ye 9, Ad 1776.

Regt. orders: The armour of the regt. is to attend
strickly to fit up ye arms of the comps. without delay. To begin att Capt. Hookers comp., then Capt.
Norton Comp., then Boldings, then Capt. Charp,
then Capt. Elderkins. These five comps. are immediately to make returns to the Agitant of what amunition is wanted to compleat them to Eightteen
rounds a man, officers included. The officers of each
Comp. are, soon as posible, to make out pay
Rowles for their respective Comp., specifying officers
and men in coloms; men's Names, times of enlistment,
when made up to number of months and days,
wayges for month and sums due. The rowles to be
made up to the 30th of Sept. and to be deliverd in
to the Col. without delay. All the sick of the Regt.,
as soon as the wether will permit, will parade in the
front of the Regt. by the Serj. of Each Comp. The
Docter will visit them and see who shall be freed from
(duty); the other must attend duty to proserve their

health. The agitant is to get a rowl or roster of the officers of the Regt. A subst. may be appoynted day by day to inspect, as officers of the day, the Aconomy of the Saveral Comp. in their cookry. The seviral sorts of clothing for the troops being sent yesterday to the general, from Yonsey, Massers and Taylor, to whom the goods Belong. Any solgiers may know the price of what they want to purchis (by) Appliing to Comesary Sickels, att the Continettol Store in the old fort. Field officer of the day tomorrow, for mount indpet, Major Brown, Brigade Major of the 3 Brigade.

Headquarters, October ye 10, Ad 1776.

General orders: The guard, for the futer, to be paraded att 9 o'clock on the grand parade. Contrary to all Displine and in Disobedience of the most Positive orders, some officers & solgiers have prosumd to shoot and other game, in & about the camp; no less than 2 officers and 28 men being yesterday detected in the above Scandilus (practice.) For their punment, The general orders the officers to oversee the men, who are all of them to be imployd two days in picking O Com (oakum) for the use of the fleet, and such as are for the futer found Gilty fireing their arms without orders are to be delt with in Like manner. Officers of the day tomorrow, for Ticonderogue, Major Rogers, Brigade major Brown; officer of the day for Mount Independent, Major More, Brigade Major, first Brigade.

Ticonderogue, Mount independant, Oct. ye 11, Ad 1776.

General orders: The Stupineness and Seeming stupinences of the Enemy straingly indecates that they are. It therefore Behovs every officer & Solgier of this army to be exceeding a Elart, particular when on duty. The officers of the day att ticonderogue, as well as Mount independence, are, by their example, to give life and spirit to the guard under their Inspection. The guard and visiting rounds are upon no Account to be Negligence of their duty; Observing to be very attentive to the Sentres and guards from 4 in the morning—broad light. As the Campaign is drawing towards the close, the general is angtious Nothing Disgracefull to the troops under his command should tarnish that good behaveour that they have hitherto shown. Field officer for ticonderogue, tomorrow, Major frazer; Brigade major not known. Field officer of the day tomorrow for mount Independent, Major Sumner, Brigade Major, 2 Brigade.

Mount independant, October the 12, Ad 1776.

Regt. orders: The commanding officers of Comp. are to see that all the men that are abel turn out and all of (off) duty to attend att roll calling in the front of the Regt. once a day and that Imediately after the *treet beting; officer Leut. Frizel.

Mount independant, October the 12, 1776.

Porowl, Sidry; Countersign, handri. Those Regt. that have taken   by general orders, to have

---

*The drum beat for the "treat" or daily allowance of liquor, immediately after which the roll was called.

them marked on the Starn, which may be distinguished from other boats. The Dischargd solgiers are to return in to the commanding officer of the Regt. to which they belong, the arms, Aecrutiments, Amination and soforth, which they have in prosction belong to the public. The Commanding officers are to see that this orders are complied with. A return of the Names, Comp. and Regt. of Solgiers who are dischargd from the servace from the first of October is to be given in to the agitant genaral at orderly time; afterwards a weekly return on Saturday. Field officer of the day tomorrow, for Ticonderogue, Col. Ward; Brigade, major Byan. Field officer of the day tomorrow, for Mount independence, Col. Morrill, Brigade Major Howell.

Mount Independence, October 13, Ad 1776.

Porole, Brutus; Countersign, Hencox. Att a general cort marshal of the first and Secont Brigade, of which Col. Marsh was Prisident, Solomon Twist, a Solgier In Capt. More's Comp., in Col. Read Regt., was tried for sleeping on his poast. The prisoner Confest the fact but it being Provd that he was sick at the time the cort do a quit him. James geres, a solgier in Capt. Sheperds comp., in Col. Porters Regt., tried for the same fact and by the same court marshal, the cort a quit the prisiner from corporal punnishment, it being proved that he had not his proper Proses att the time of his committing the crime, but ajudge that he be one month out of his pay —for the use of the sick of the Regt.,—and all the expences of being Aprihended by the cort. Ensn Benjaman Carno, of Col. Warter's Regt., tried by the same cort marshal, for neglect of duty and neglect of orders, is found gilty of Disobedience of orders & sentensed To be Dischargd of servace. Ensn Whitmor, late of Col. Reed's Regt., tried by the same court marshal for behaveing unworthy of an officer or a solgier or gentleman, and Contirary to the Express resolvd of Congress, Publishd in general orders, the 5 of September, last, is found Gilty and sentensed to suffer the punishment in said Resolvd, to viz: To forfit one month pay for the use of the sick of the Regt., and be Dismist from the servis with Infamy. Leut. Abby, of the orgratons Regt., tried by the same cort marshal for acting in a sutler's business in selling bear in camp, is found gilty of a breach of general orders, September last, and sentensed. The punishments above ordered by 24. John Pratt, Ensn of the same Regt., tried by the same court marshall, & for the same crime, is found gilty and sentensed to Received the same punishment. Joseph Marcome, a solgier of Capt. Harpor's Comp., in Col. Warnors Regt., tried by the same court marshal for stealling, found gilty and sentensed to receivd 39 stripes on his naked body at the head of the Regt. Joseph Slumona, a solgier of Capt. Drawers' Comp., in Col. Waymons Regt., tried by the same court Marshall for stealling a pocket book and for cursing the officers of the guard, is found gilty of both crimes, is sentensed to receivd 39 stripes on naked back first and 20 lashes for the 2 offence at the head of the Brigade he belongs to. The general approvd of the proseedings and orders all the sentensed to take place Amediately, Punctually. Those (penalties) put on the officers who are orderd to leave the Camp amediately after Dischargd (discharging) there (their) Dets. The general cort marshal, of (which) Leut. Col. marsh was president, is desolvd. The Regtall(regimental)Surgeon are to deliver att the medical store all the lint that have got made att 6 o'clock this afternoon, one orderly Serj. from each Regt. & a man from the artilery to attend Constant att head quarters. Field officer of the day tomorrow, for ticonderogue, Col. Woodbredge; Brigade Major Byan. Field officer of the day for mount independent, Col. Wingate, Brigade Major of the 3 Brigade.

Mount independece, October 14, Ad 1776.

Regt. orders: The Serj. of the quarter guard is to Padrole the Sentres in the midle of the time between each relief from midnight to sunrise till futher orders. As the enemy is ourly expected an atack this Camp, itt is expected the Regt. under arms every morning at 4 o'clock, and repair with all silence to the alaraming poast & stand there till Broad day light. The officers and men see that their arms and amanition are at hand that they may take them at any moment in the Night.

SAMUEL MOOT,

Col.

Head quarters, Ticonderogue, Oct. the 14, Ad 1776.

Porowl, Warterbury; countersign, Wiglesworth. Leut. peter Hews of the First Battallion of Pensilvanians, is (to) act as Adicamp to general gates during the absence of major Warters' steward. As every Regt. and Corps are well acquainted with allaraming poast, the general expects the troops will be Elark (on the alert) to support the works they severally intend to defend. He has the most dependance on the bravery of the troops and beliefs that if cald to action they will shew themselves worthy of the couse they are engagde to defend. He returns his harty thanks to General Arnold, officers, seman and marines of the fleet for the Galant Defence they made against the Superority of the Enemy. More such Brave behavour Will Establish the fame of American arms Throughout the Globe. Capt. Leut. Gibstones has taken the command of Artiliry on Mount independent. Officer of the day tomorrow for Ticonderogue, Col. Woodbredge, Brigade major Byan. officer of the day for mount independant, Col. Wingate, Brigade Major the 1 Battilion.

October the 15, 1776.

As there is not intrenching tools to imploy The Solgiers on duty, the general Expects the officers of duty and the Col. of the Regt. will order one third of the men off duty to parade att 7 OClock every morning for fatigue, who are to be kept at work till 10 oclock in the fornoon, one third more to Relief att 10 who are To work till one in the afternoon, the other third to Relieve them and work till 5 in Even; these to be constently and Regularly Untill counter orders. The general is unhapy to See the wont of that Spirit and Elartness and indistry So Nesasary for Prasivation of the provails in this army. The fleet has acted a nobil part—Let itt Not be Said that the cause of all Amarica by the supineness of the Northern Army. Capt. Jones on the Side of ticonderogue and Major Bigelow will Resume the command of Artilary on Mount independant. Field officer of the (day) tomorrow, for ticondergue, Lieut. Col. Ogden; Brigad major Brown. field officer of the day for mount independant, Col. Swift, Brigade major 2 Battalion.

Mount Independants, October 16, *Ad* 1776.

Regt. orders: The commanding officers of the comps. are to take Proticular care of all the tents in their camp, that they are kept clean, unhurt, that they may Serve another campaign and A vandue to be held this day, to Begin att 10 o'clock at Capt. Stephen's House for the sale of the Efecks of Some Desiest Solgier. Any one Enclined to purchase may attend.

Headquarters, Ticonderogue, October 16, Ad 1776.

Porowl, falmouth. A general court marshall of the lines of which Brigadear General Saint Clear was president. Capt. Jonathan and John tasset. Leut. Rufis pary, Jonathan Wright, Mathew Lyon, were tried For Deserting their poast on inion River without being attackd by the enemy and without orders. The court have duly considered the evidence for and against and are of opinion that Capt. Jonathan & John tasset, Leut. John Wright & Leut. Lyon are gilty of leaving their poast without orders or without being Attack or forst by the Enemy & They judge that Leut. Rufus pary, gilty of a breach (of) the 6 artical of the rule and regulation published by the continctal congress for the Better regulation of the army, and doo judge that Capt. Jonathan Tasset and Capt. John Tassett, Leut. John Wright, Leut.

Rufis pary and Leut. Mathew Lion be Dischargd and forfit all their pay, to be apropriated towards making good the damage substaind by the Inhabitants on Inion river on account of their unsolgier Like behavior and that they be, each of them are casheard, to be inCapible of Ever Hereafter holding military, comisind or imployment in the states of Amarica and that their names and crimes be publishd in the news papers and Serj. Phenihas Ripley, Corp. Jonathan Whitteleser, Jabez Armistead, Reuben Baker, John Welch, Samuel Smith, Daniels Addams, Constant Randal, Zacariah Homes, Jonathan pary, George Owles, Rufuss Bates, Ezeriah Brooks, Elisha Starkwether, William Howland, Amos Faset, Bigmon Homes, Ephraham Smith, Edward Summers, tried by the same courtmarshal for meeting. The cort, after deliberation, are of opinion that Corp. Wittleser and Baker, Welch, Smith, Rendwells, Owles, Bates, Brooks, Starkwether, Howell, Homes, are guilty of meeting. That Serj. penihas Ripley, David Addams, Homes, Smith, are not gilty and judge that Corp. Whitlesee to be reduced to the ranks and receive 39 lashes on his naked back, and Samuel Smith 39 lashes on his bareback, and Amos Fasset 39 lashes, and all picken oakam; the other all to receive 20 Lashes on their Naked back att such place as the general shall appoint, & be kept a week picken oakom. The general approves of the Above Sentences and orders those of the officers to take place immediately. Those on the solgiers to be put in execution, that in the corporal ponishment, when the guard is releived and after the deputy quartermaster general will direct their Imployment.

the general court marshal, of which general St. Clear was president, is Desolved. Field officer of the day tomorrow, for Ticonderogue, Leut. Col. Cragg; Brigade Major Byan. Field officer of the day for Mount independent, Col. Mott; Brigade Major Howel.

October the 17, Ad 1776.

Poreul, Mongomary. The comesary is Emediately to isue out half a gill of rum to Every Non comisind officer and solgier now in camp, and should the wet weather hold till evining he is (to) issue one half gill more. A Deteachment of a Capt., 3 subs., 3 Serjs., and on (one) Hundred Rank & file to parade as soon as posible from Col. Brewar's and Col. Willard's Regt. with axes, who are to proseed to cut trees across the Crount (Crown) point Road. the quarter-master of each Regt. to deliver all their spare tents Belonging to their respective corps to Col. Morgin Lewis, Deputy quartermaster general, att 4 o'clock this after Noon. Col. Lewis will give his receipt for the same. Mr. Robert Hops is appointed quarter master of the first Battalion of pensylvanians In the room of Quartermaster Nickels, and John King is appointed Ensign in the room of Mr. Coy, dead, in the same battalion of Pensylvanians. Field officer of the day tomorrow, for tieonderoguega, Leut. Col. Brown; Brigade Major Brown. Field officer of the day tomorrow, Leut. Col. Marsh; Brigade major th first Battalion.

Headquarters, Ticonderoguega, Oct. ye 18, Ad 1776.

General orders: The comesary to supply all the

emty casks he has in the store that will hold water, to such Regts. as has not water conveneant to their Elaraming Post. They are to be kept filld with pure water that the troops may have a supply ready when wanted. A quantity rum also to be handy, to be (issued) when allowed, when ordered, as the enemy can have no resenable hopes of Destroying this army unless the troops poasted in the redoutes and the advanced guard suffer themselves to be supprisd. The Genll. strongly recomends it to all the officers and solgiers to exart themselves with the utmost vigulence while on duty, Never omitting the smallist attendance to the approach of the enamy, and giving them the most vigorous opposition to every attempt. Col. Marshfield, without delay, to joyn Col. win's Regt. on the side of Ticonderogue. The ground of their encampment will be shewn by the Debuty Quartermaster gen. The comesary is emediately to isue out half a gill of rum to every non comisind officer and solgier now in camp, att 1 o'clock this after Noon. the genll. expects an exact obedience to these orders respecting the delivery of all the spare tools to the debuty quartermaster genll. 2 Regts. yet have not done their duty according to that order. Field officer of the day tomorrow, for ticonderogue, Leut. Col. Lenard; Brigade Major Rion. Field officer for Mount independance, Leut. Col. Sherve; Brigade major 2 Brigade.

After orders: The comesary to deliver 5 sheep to each regt. as early as posible tomorrow morning. The artiliry & corps. of Artificers to receive 4 sheep Each, These are to Recon in the allowance of provition att their estimated weights.

Headquarters, October the 19, 1776.

Leut. Col. Baldin, first Enginear, will take the Derection of the works on the side of Ticonderoguega with the following asistants under him: major pinn, Capt. Newlin, Leut. Doglis, Ensn Parret; Leut. Col. philiser, Second Enginear, will take derection of the works on this side of mount independence, with the following assistance of Capt. Patison Dubiany and any two getelmen that the Col. on that side recomands. This arangment being Setled, Particular works to be accomplished determined upon, the general has no Dought but the Necesary Preparations For a vigorores attept, Defence will be with that anemated ziele becoming solgiers who are also free Citysons of Amarica. Such non comisind officers & solgiers whose arms have bin wet in the late bad weather and can not be drawn are to be drawn up in quadrian in proper places half an hour before sunrise and then Discharge them. The Regts. who want amunition may Be Supplyed by applying to Col. Trumbull, debuty Agatant general. The comesary is to deliver all the emty casks on this side Lake to the order of Col. Wane, who will be derected where to place them. The troops to have 4 days provision constantly drest till Farther orders. All the spears that can be speard (spared) from the on board the shipping, to be deliverd for the defence of the french lines and redoupts. The comanding officer of artiliry will prove and seale such guns as wanted, at the same time try one to fire. Field officer of the day for Ticonderoguega, Leut. Col. Brigade major Rion. Field officer for Mount independence, Leut. Col. Caror; Brigade Major Howel.

Headquarters, Ticonderoguega, the 20, Ad 1776.

Field officer of the day for Ticonderoguega, Leut. Col. Robards; Brigade Major Rion. Field officer for Mount independent, Leut. Col. Sentor; brigade major of the first brigade. The princibill asistant engincar being sick, by the yesterday's orders, no person is to direct any new works or repair any old works, without first Receiving the engincar's Approbation and order for the same. As it is unsertin of which of our poasts the enemy may make their attack, the general desires and expects that the officers and men fit for duty in the Regts. on both sides of the lake hold themselves in rediness to march or embark for what ever place or part of the camp may need their support. Agitant Hunt Cole, of Bond's Regt., is ordered to do the duty of Major of Brigades To the first brigade on Mount Independent. During the sickness of major Howel, Agitant Walker to do the duty in the secont brigade in the absence of Major Rice.

Ticonderoguega, October the 21, Ad 1776.

General orders: The following arangment of surgeons in this army is to take place in case of action: Doct. Canaiday, Barnet, Taylor, Jacson, Silby, Picher, to attend att the old foort with their Mates. Doct. Johnson, homes, Elisson, harvy, Stuard, with their mates. Col. Maxwell's Battalion is to joyn & doo duty with General St. Clear's Brigade. Mr. William McHardra is appointed Agitent of Col. Makoi's (McCoy) Brigade in place of Agitant Johnson. A guard of a Serjt. and 12 privates to mount this evening. The Batiries which (are) placed near the cove under mount independent, on the west side, this guard to suffer no boats to be taken without a written order from the commanding officer of brigade or from headquarters or the quartermaster genll. Field officer of the (day) tomorrow for Ticonderoguega, Major Dhart; Brigade major Brown. Field officers for mount independent, Leut. Col. Starr; Brigade Major Walker.

Head quarters, Ticonderoguega, Oct. 22, Ad 1776.

Capt. Tobias Janald, of Col. Phines' Regt., is orderd to do the duty of Major in that Regt. in the absence of Major Brown, sick. Whereas, if a action happens on Ticonderoguega side, the wounded, after being dressed att the place in yesterday's orders, are to be caried to Doct. Potty, att the general Hospitial on the mount. The boats will be kept constantly ready att the carpender shop in the cove for this purpas. Col. Maxwell Waines, Col. Hearvey's Battallion, are to furnish major Stephens of artiliry, with such men with the non comisind officers for the artiliry servis. Genll. Bricket's brigade to furnish 30 men and an officer for the same purpis. They are to bring their camp kittle from the Regt. Tents will be furnished for them. The 2 Jersey battilion are to do duty in camp with other battilion of the brigade, but they are still to be employed in their own alarm poast, ownly (except) the party wanted for the artiliry. Field officer for Ticonderoguega, Major Butler; Brigade major Rion. Field officer for Mount independent, Leut. Col. Worthington; Brigade major Howel.

The genll. strongly recomends it to all the officers

44

and solgiers to exart themselves with the utmost
vigilance while on duty, never omitting the
smallist attendention to the abroach of the enemy
and giving them the most vigurous opposition to
every attempt. Col. Marsh's & Col. Win's Regts.,
without delay, to have the side of Ticonderoguega.
The ground of their encampment will be shown by
the debuty quartermas general. The comesary to
issue out Emediately half a gill of rhum to every non
comisind officer and solgier now in camp, at 1
o'clock this afternoon. The genll. expects exact obedience to these orders, and of yesterday, respecting the
delivery of all the spare tools (to) the debuty Quar.
genll. Field officer for the day tomorrow, for Ticonderoga, Leut. Col. Lonard; Brigade major Rion.
Field officer for mount ind., Leut. Col. Sherve; Brigade major 2 brigade.

Head quarters, Ticonderogucga, Oct. 23, Ad 1776.

The genll. court marshall from the 2 brigades of
which Genll St. Clear and Bracets, set tomorow morning at the president's tent, for the tryal of such prisoners as may be brought before them. President, Leut.
Col. Bragg: members, 12 captains. Field officer of
the day tomorrow, for Ticonderoguega, Major Frasier; Brigade major Brown. Field officer for Mount
independent, Major Sherborn; Brigade major Hunt.
For guard, 5 men; for fatigue, 5 men.

Headquarters, Ticonderoguega, Oct. the 24, Ad 1776.

The commanding officers of Regts. are Direcly to
draw ¼ quarter of a pound of buck shot for every
man fit for duty in their respective comps. The hon-

ble, the congress of the United States have, for the reward and incuragement of every non comisind officers & solgier who shall Ingage to serve during the war, further resolved to give over and above the bounty, 20 dollers to each man annually, one compleat suite of cloaths which, for the present year, is to consist of 2 linnd hunting shirts, 2 pair of stockings, 2 pair of shoes, 2 pair of hoverhawls, a leather or woollin jacket with sleeves, 1 pair of breaches & 1 leather cap or hat, or that sum to be payd to each solgier who shall provide those articles for himself and produce a cirtifocate thereof from the Capt. of the Comp. to which he belongs, to the paymaster of the Regt. This, a Noble bounty of 40 dollars and one Hundred acers of Land, att the end of the war, is such an ample and generous gratuaty from the united States that the general is not concernd that no American will hesitate to enrole himself to defend his contry and property from every attempt. Field officer of the day tomorrow, Major Stacey; Brigade major Rion. Field officer for Mount independent, Major Cilly; Brigade major Watter. For guard, 5 men; for fatigue, 5 men.

October the 25, Ad 1776.

Col. Mott's order: That the sutlers tending of the 2 Coneticut Regts. are not to sell any spirettis liquor to any person except the men of ye above 2 Regt., except to the main guard, nor them without an order from the Capt. of the guard. If the sutler of the 2 Regt., and by that means, the men are drunk and unfit for duty, the sutler or those that attend the store are gilty of this, shall be subject to such pun-

ishment as the marshal law will inflict. The
sutlers is not to sell any of the following artickels at
more than the prices herein stated, vis: Good West-
india, * 4s for quort, 2s : 0 : 2 for point, 1 : 0 : 2 for
half point, 8 for gill; tenarief wine, 5s for quort;
Jameca spirets, 5s : 0 : 0 quort, good french Brandy
5s : 0 : 0 quort; geneva of the best kind, 3s : 0 : 0
for point; comon rhum, 3s : 9 for quort; Loofe
suger at 3s : 0 for pound; vinagor, 1s : 4 for quort;
Raysons, 2s : 0 for pound; coffee, 2s : 0 for pound.
These prises to be attended too till further orders.

Head quarters, October 27, Ad 1776.

As the enemy's attack will more probily be suden,
the genll. most Earnistly recomends it to every comisind officer of his Regt., part, poast or detachment,
to be delebirate and cool in sufring his men to fire,
never allowing them to throw away his shot in an
unsolgier like maner. One close and well derected
fire att the distant of eight or ten rods will doo more
towards defeeting the enemy than all the scaterd
random shots will doo in a whole day. The com-
ander of the artiliry will give all proper derection under his comand. The affect of this observa-
tion of this order will, of the blessings of heaven,
secure the victury. The comesary will isue half
a gill of rhum to every non comisind officer &
solgier now in camp, fit for duty att 2 o'clock this
afternoon. All officers who mount guard are to ap-
pear at the brigade and to march them to the parade. The corps which have not drew their shot
acording to order are to send in their return emediately and receivd the same as each corps make their

---

quorter masters of Regts. will issue to the men att
their elarm poast in the morning.

Head Quorters, October the 31, Ad 1776.

The comesary is for the futer to issue 1 pound and
half of beef to each man & a pound of flour till further orders. The rations hetherto issued the comesary are to be made good and payed by him as soon
as the demand ean be ajusted. Field officer for
mount independent, Col. Swift; Brigade Major
Hunt; agitant of the day, Convis. The whole of the
troops to have 3 days' provition redy drest. For
guard, 7 men; for fatigue, 7 men.

Head quorters, November the 1, Ad 1776.

Field officer of the day, Col. Mott; Brigade major
Walker. Agitant of the day tomorow, Mr. Warner.
For guard, 7 men, and 6 men for fatigue.

Head Quorters, November the 2, Ad 1776.

The Regts. of Reed's, Graton's and Poor's are Immediately upon A General Alarm to repair to ticonderoguega. Col. Doughton's regiment are to ocopy
the old foort and such Regts. as have sick, they must
move them as soon as posible. Capt. John B. Scott,
of Col. Maxwell's Regt., tryed by A genll. court marshal, of which Col. Cragg is president, for defrauding
the United States of America by presenting a falce
pay rowle and receivd his pay acordingly; for the un-
getleman like behavour, Extorting Extroardaly price
for some artickles purchashed for his men & for dis-
chargeing solgiers without the Col's Leaf. The cort,
on considering the effidences, find Capt. Scoot gilty

of defrauding the United States by Prosenting a false pay rowle and drawing the pay acordingly & also of ungentleman like behavour in extorting extreordely prices for some Artickles purchised for his men and do sentence him to be casheheird and repay all ye overpluss money containd in the pay rowle. Capt. parker, Leut. Cheney and Leut. Osborn of Col. Reed's Regt., tryed (for) disobedience of orders, are found not gilty and, acordingly, Equited them with onner. The genll. approved of ye above Sentence and orders them to take place Immediately, as also the Sentence of Capt. Daniels and Leut. Whitney, where Entred in the orders of the 29 olt and omited to be approved att that time, they are to take place Im-mediately. John Brown, a solgier in Capt. mikin's Comp. in Col. Wine's Regt., tryed by the same genll. courtmarshal, all found gilty, is sentensed to receive 78 lashes on his bare Back. The genll. approvd the above sentence and orders them to be executed att such time & place as the commanding officer of the Regt. shall think proper. The fatigue on mount in-dependent the same as was ordered 31 of October. Field officer of the day on ye mount, Leut. Col. Marsh; Brigade major Howel; agitant of the day, Mr. Con-vis. For guard, 6 men and 1 serjt., and for fatigue, 6 men.

Head Quorters, Nov. 3, Ad 1776.

James Moris Jones is appointed ensn in Col. Shold's Battalion. Att a genll. court marshal of the 3 Brig-ades on mount independent, of which Col. pheney was president, Mical migee, A Solgier in Capt. Downs' comp., in Col. Burrel's Regt., tryed for abuse-

ing and thretning the life of Alen McDaniels, found
not gilty and Equited by the court. Ebenezer foot
and George Errison, solgiers in Col. Burise's Regt.,
tryed by the same court for leaving their poasts
when on sentry and getting A Sleep, are found gilty
of breach of 23 artickle of the Rule of the army & are
sentents to receive 20 lashes each on their bare back.
Leut. Walingford, in Col. Winegates' Regt., tryed by
the same court Marshall above mentined, for ungentleman like behavor and complaining that Capt.
Bager had cheated His Comp., and Encurigeing the
Deserting of Daniel Kan and for leaving his arest; they
have duly considerd the effidences in the case and
are of oppinion that Leut. Wallingford (is guilty) of A
Breach of ye 49 Artickle of the army and sentents
him to be dischargd from the army. The genll. approvd of all the above sentenses and orders that
they take place immediately. Field officer for mount
independent, Leut. Col. Buel; Brigade Major Hunt;
agitant of the day, Warner. For guard, 7 men; for
fatigue, 6 men.

Head Quorters, November the 4, Ad 1776.

Field officer for mountindependent, Leut. Col. Cen-
ter; Brigade Major Walker. 6 men for guard, 1
serj; 6 men for fatigue.

Head Quorters, November the 5, Ad 1776.

Col. Wine is orderd to Imbark tomorow morning
for Skeensborough with such non comisind officers
and solgiers of the first New Jersey Battalion whose
times of Establishment is Exspired and who are to
be dischargd amediately. They will Imbark att 3

o'clock, 5 men in each boate. They are to return in all their Aminition that has been deliverd out to them, this afternoon, to the quortermaster of the Regt., who will deliver in the whole when colected, to the comesary of artiliry. Such officers, non comisind officers and solgiers of the first Jersey Battalion as have an atachment to their genll. & a zeal for the servis of their Contry and are Wiling to remain in camp until the 15 of Novmber shall, then be promited to depart with honour & be alowed pay for their return home. Josiah Remnant, A solgier in Capt. Blisses Comp., in Col. Patison's Regt., tryed by a general courtmarshall, of which Col. phency was president, tryed for Sleeping on his poast, is found gilty & sentants to be Whipt 20 lashes on his bare back. Ye genll. approvd of the sentents but upon the request of the court and Recomendation & onesty and good Behaver of the Crimenal Every Instant till this, he is pleased to grant his pardon and orders the prisiner to be releasd. The genll. att the same time assures the army as this was the first itt shall be the last instants of his pardening A crime so dangeros as this sleeping on his poast. The court of which Col. phency was president is desolved. Col. Start will order all the men off duty in his Brigade and such of the Malisha as are able to asist to give every aide in their power to finish the palisadin the new fort and the Appatee (abatis) Round it. Field officer of the day for mount indep., Leut. Col. Starr; Brigade Major Howel; agitant of the day, Convis. For guard, 7 men; for fatigue, 6 men.

Head Quorters, November the 6, Ad 1776.

The genll. derects that each Regt. and corps. cut and fetch their own fire wood for a few days till the A. D. Q. G. Colect a sufishent quontity to begin ensuing (issuing) that artickles in A proper manner. Boats and axses will be furnished those that want them for that purpis. In the mean Time the guard, the wood guard is to suffer no officers nor solgiers to take any wood without a written order from A. D. Q. G., major Hay. 2 Leut. downer is appointed 1 Leut. to the comp. of Pensylvanians artiliry, vice Leut. Willow, resind 2; 2 Leut. Barr to be 2 Leut., vise Leut. donet, advanced; Leut. Colwell, Conductor, to be 2, 2 Leut. Barr, advanced. James Beety, a solgier in Capt. Hanege's comp., in Col. Whitcom's Regt., tryed by a genaral court marshal, of which Leut. Col. Cragg was president, appeald from a Regt., is aquited. Zelida Hammon, mate; William Pownwell, Boatswain; William trip & Nicolas Culbut, seamen of the fleet, tryed by the same genll. courtmarshal for mutiny, in wishing that the enemy would come and saying that they would not fite them on board the vessels, found gilty and sentenced: Zelida, mate, to be broke and return to his former Regt. and doo private's duty; Pownwell to receive 98 lashes on his bare back and doo duty as a private In his former Regt.; trip & Colbut to receive each 78 lashes on their bare back and Return to their former duty on board. The genll. approvd of their proseedings and orders the corporal punishment to be inflicted this afternoon. The crimonals to be whipt from vessel to vessel in receiving part of their punishment from each. Field officer for Mount independent,

Leut. Col. Worthington; Brigade Major Hunt; agitant of the day, Mr. Crane. For guard, 7 men; for fatigue, 4 men & 1 serj.

Head quorters, November the 7, Ad 1776.

The genll. returns his thanks to the officers and solgiers of the first New Jersey Battalion who remain, with warmth, for the honour and public spiret they Shewd in disdaining to follow the ill Example of their Col. and the Deluded solgiers that acompinyde him, yesterday. The genll. would inform them that the drums was beat by his order in derision of the few who had the baseness to quit their post in this time of danger. The battoes guard to be increased to 1 sub. & 21 Privates. They are to keep sentiries over the wood as well as the boats. Field officer of the day for mount independant, major Shermon; Brigade major Walker; agitant of the day, Warner. 6 men for guard and 3 men for fatigue.

Head Quorters, November 8th, Ad 1776.

The major of Brigades will be perticular careful that the Weekly return Tomorow will be very corect, noting all Alteration sence Last Return, all vacanses and absents of officers. The Col. of Mulitisha is to deliver in to the D. A. G. att ordaly time tomorow an exact return of their corps. Field officer for the Mount, Major Silly. Brigade major Howell; agitant of the day, Convis. For guard, 5 men and 3 men for fatigue.

Head quorters, Ticonderoguega, Nov. 9th, Ad 1776.

Field officer of the day for ye mount, Major Hale;

Brigade Major Hunt. The following promotions are to take place in Col. Poor's Regt.: 2 Leut. Nathan Maclantick is appointed Agitant; Ensn Culver to be 2 Leut., Leut. persons, dead; Serjt.-quarter master, Ensn, * Leut. Culver advanced; 2 Leut. Hunting, 1 Leut., Leut. Matthias, Cashierd; Ensn pike, 2 Leut., Leut. Rinling advanced; Serjt. major Front, ensn, Ensn pike advaneed. Agitant of ye day, Warner. For guard, 5 men and 3 men for fatigue.

Head Quorters, November the 10, Ad 1776.

As a vain of black flint stone being descoverd on mountindep. the genll. Desires the commanding officers of Regts. will make inquiry if there be any old contry man in any of their corps. who understands hammering gun flints, they will be sent to head quorters. The general court marshall now setting are to try the officers & solgiers acused of killing Mr. Adams ox. Mr. Adams and Mr. Davis & the Effidences are to be Summonsed to attend the court. Agitant of the day, Mr. Crain. For guard, 5 men; for fatigue, 3 men.

Head quorters, Ticonderoguega, November the 11, Ad 1776.

The following promotions are ordered to take place in the 2 Pensylvanian Battallion: 1 Leut. Samuel more, Capt., Capt. Cragg, promoted; 1 Leut. James Carter, capt., Capt. Butler, promoted; 2 Leut. Roos,

---

* This evidontly means that the quartormaster-sergeant (whose name was not givon) was made ensign in place of Ensign Culver who had been advanced to 2d Lieutenant.

1 Leut., Leut. Moirster, advanced; 2 Leut. Henry
Epple, 1 Leut., Leut. Chelton, resind; Ensn James
Armstrong, 2 Leut., Leut. Curac, advanced; Ensn
George Hafner, 2 Leut., Leut. Cragg, advanced; Ensn
marshall, 2 Leut., Leut. Epple, advanced; Mr. Abner
Dun, ensn, Ensn Armstrong, advanced. Field officer
of the day for Mount, Major More; Brigade major
Howel. Agitant of the day, Mr. Convis. 5 men for
guard and 3 men for fatigue.

Head Quorters, November the 12, Ad 1776.

Leut. Col. White, Capt. Patison & Capt. Gordin,
of Col. Doles' Regt., tried by a general court Marshal held att malbyny (Albany), whereof Capt. Van-
Shroak was president, of being concerned in the embez-
elment of sertin —— belonging to John Johnson. The
court, after due examanation, are of opinion that the
charge against the Prisenors was groundless, aquit
them (with) honour. His Exsilensa, General Washington, has approved of the Proceedings of the court
and orders this testimony of his approbation be in-
serted in genll. orders in the Nothern army. No officer of any corps, whatsoever, is to recount from
the Regt. commanded By Col. Patison. Major Hay,
Capt. Bush, of the 6 Pensylvanian Battallion, Mr.
Sickels of the 1 Jersey battallion are appointed to
settle the prises of goods brought from Canada; that
the Regt. to reserve the Said goods, that they may
be able to settle their acounts & payments for them.
The genll. court marshall, of which Leut. Col. Cragg
was president, is desolved. Field officer for the
mount, Shegwick; Brigade major Howel; Agitant,
Warner.

Head quorters, November 13th, Ad 1776.

The first Battallion of Pensylvanians and first 2 of the Jersey Regts. are to be taken of (off) duty & prepair to embark for foort George as soon as the Battoas are ready that will be Appointed to cary Them over the lake. Ye Commanding officers of Regts. will Be Answerable for any damage done to any of the huts or building belonging to their Corps. The troops that return home be careful to proserve every thing that can, in the least degree, be usefull to those that tary here. Those Corps that leave their arms, to return in all their amunition to the comesary of artiliry. The guards are to be lessend by a detail given to major of Brigade this day. Field officer for the mount independents, Major Sumner; Brigade major Walker. For guard, 5 men, and for fatigue, 3 men.

Mountindependents, November 14th, Ad 1776.

Regt. orders: A return of the arms and acutriments (accouterments) that belong to the public, of the men who have died in the saviral compinies and those which are privates' property and have no owner to carry them home, is to be given to the Col. Emediately, spacifying the number of each by their march billeting rowl. (Sums due) dew to the saviral Comps. from the time of their enlistment to the time they Marchd, are to be made out without delay & given in and also the sums dew each Comp. yet unpayd, for the transportation of their bagage, and acounts of what is due to every comp. for marching through the contry acording to Proclamation. The quorter master is without delay to see that the Acounts are made up to the 31 of October of all such arears of money for rations, & So as money thats due to the Regts., and make due application for the pay. The Commanding officers of the seviral compinies are to take care to keep accounts of all the Deffirent dates of who are dischargd of the Difirent men who are Dischargd, that the pay may be stopt in from ye pay rowl att a proper time.

SAMUEL MOTT, Col.

For guard, 1 serjt. and 6 men.

Head quorters, November the 14, Ad 1776.

Col. Rechars' 1 and 2 Jersey Battallion to Embark tomorow morning by sunrise for foort George. The genll. thanks all the officers & Solgiers of those Regts. now on this ground for their Rediness and complying with his request to remain this week for the defence of this post after their time of servis was exspired. The genll., in particular manner, acknowledges the good servis of Major Deheart, and the officers & solgiers of the 1 Jersey Regt. who had the Honour not to follow their Col. to the winter quorters. Col. Graton and Col. Bond & Col. porter's Regts., to Enbark (for) foort George tomorow After noon, provided they are then A sofitient Number of Battoes to transport them over the Lake. Such artificers that Belong to any of the Corps. going to winter quorters as these (and) are willing to remain in this post till the Barracks are Finished, Col. Bollding, chief Ingenear, will pay and discharge them when Business so Nesasary to the public is finished. Field officer for the Mount, Col. Phiney; Brigade major Hunt. For guard, 6 men.

Head quorters, November the 15, Ad 1776.

Capt. Sylson's Comp. of Rifell men is to be Joyned & act With the 4 Battallion Pensylvanians, Commanded by Col. Wine. Col. Graton, Late Col. Bon's and Col. Porter's Regts. are not to march till further orders. Cols. Stark & Poor's, & Read's, Regts., will be ready to march tomorow morning att 8 o'clock to the Landing at Lake George, where the bouts are ready to cary them over the lake. Field officer for the mount, Col.   ; Brigade Major Walker. 6 men for guard.

Head quorters, November 16th, Ad 1776.

Any Non comisind officer and solgier inlisted from the Regt., who have Ingaged to serve till ye last of December, are not to have furloughs before the present time of servis is exspird, but who are inlisted from the 10 Regts. of malisha, whose servis is exspired the last day of this month, shall emediately receive furloughs from the commanding officer that they are Engaged in, for one month from the date of said furlough. This to be a standing order not to be departed from. A genll. court marshal on the 2 Brigade, on Ticonderoguega side, to set tomorow morning att 9 o'clock, att the president's tent, for ye tryal of such prisoners as shall be Brought before them. The president, Col. Woods; the Members, 2 field officers and 12 Captains, an agitant and an ordalay Serjt. from the 2 Brigade. Field officer for the mount, Col. Wayman; Brigade Major Hunt. 5 men for guard.

Head quorters, November the 17, Ad 1776.

Col. Graton's, the late Col. Bon's & Col. Porter's

Regts. are to march tomorow to foort George, where the boats are ready for their Emediate Imbarcation. Capt. Joseph Blunfield, of Col. Daton's Regt., Is appointed Debaty Judg advocate of the army. Col. Wood being Uonwell, Lcut. Col. Loyrell, for a while, is appointed in his place. Field officer for the mount independents, Col. Swift; Brigade major Walker. For guard, 1 corp. & 6 privates.

Head quorters, November the 18, Ad 1776.

The following Regiments are to hold themselves in Rediness to march & embark att Lake George as soon as the Boats are Prepard for them: 1 Devision, Patison's, Phenies & Biddell Regts.; 2 Devision, Reads & Wigleworth Regts.; 3 Devision, Whelocks and Woodbredges Regts.; 4 Devision, Brewars & Willards; 5 Devision, Motts and Swift Regts.; 6 Devision, Winegaits & Wayman's Regts., to march by the Shortest & best Rode to the state of New Hampshire. Col. Anthony Wane will take the command of the Regt., of the Regts. artiliry and artificers, which are to compleat the garison of Ticonderogucga & mount-independence. Mical Ryon, Esq., is appointed brigade major for Ticonderogucga & mountindependence, & to be obayed as such. The Col. will order Major Fosse, Frasier, Capt. Homes, Capt. Bomer to aprise, on oath, all the artickles of cloathing in the garison of ticonderogucga Belonging to ye United States and order the same to be deliverd to George Masen, Esq., comesary genll. of cloathing, taking his receipt for the same, which is to be deliverd to Col. Wane, to be by him sent to the office in Philadelphia, prosnant to an order of congress. The clarks of difirent stores of dry goods are to attend to this account. Col. Daton to march with Leut. Col. Whit, under an arest for attemting to assisinate Mr. Verick, Debuty muster Master Geull., near head quorters. Field officer for ticonderoguega, Col. Reed; Brigade Major Field. Officer for the mount, Col. Swift.

Head quorters, November the 19, Ad 1776.

An ordaly book has been taken from head quorters through a mistake. Who ever has itt is desired to return itt Emediately to the brigade major. Field officer for the mount, Leut. Col. Buel. A captain of Col. Waynes, Late harwines, Woods, Brewars, Whitcoms Regts., to wait on Mr. Verrick,* Debuty Muster master genll., tomorow morning at 10 o'clock att his quorters in the garison, for derection to the capt. for his respective corps to prepare muster rowles for the comps. Emediately. The commandirs of these parties are to emediately cause their respective quorter masters to make return of such cloathing as may be wanted for solgiers, to major Masons, who will deliver on the order of the commander of the Regt. Col. Bolding will attend the working party tomorow morning. Major hay Will git as many exes this evening as he can in Rediness for his party.

Head quorters, November 20th, Ad 1776.

Porowl, Gates; countersign, Arnold. A court of inquiary to set att 10 o'clock this morning in the

* Richard Varick (late captain in Col. McDougall's regiment, which office he has resigned), secretary to the Hon. Maj. Gen. Schuyler, was appointed Deputy Muster Master General to the Northern Army, Sept. 25, 1776, by a Resolution of Congress. Journal N. Y. Provincial Congress, Vol. 2, page 347.

president's room, to inquire into ye matter of charge against Mr. crow of the fleet ; president, Major Barber. All evidences and persons concernd are to attend. Leut. Col. White having waged his honour not to challing or offer any violence to Capt. Verrick, muster master genll. to this army, until their friends have an oppertunity of setling the unhappy dispute in an honourable maner. Leut. Col. White is Releasted from the arest by the Hon. maj. genll. Gates. Col. Wayman & Col. Wingaites will hold their Regts. in rediness to march tomorow morning by way of Oter Crick road, their amanition to be returned in first to the parson who has the care of artiliry stores. Ensn John Harper to doo duty of an agitant in ye 4 Battallion of Pensylvanians, commanded by Col. Wane. Ensn phurbs to (do) duty of quortermaster in Sd (said) Regt. Officer of the day, a captain from Col. Buret's Regt. For guard, 2 men, and the rest for fatigue.

Head quorters, Nov. the 21, Ad 1776.

Porowl, Washington; countersign, Lee. The unsogier & disordaly way of firing muskets in & about the camp has bin as common that the most Examplary punishment is absolutely nesisary to provent itt. Itt is Col. Wane's orders that any one being deteced in fireing his peace shell receive 100 lashes att the head of his Regt. No Regt. under marching orders are to be excused from duty without punctual orders for that purpus. The commanding officers of those Regt. now marhing, orders will on no account whatever take away those artificers whose times of establishment is not expired till the publick is compleated & then will be payd and dischargd agreeable

63

to genll. orders. Officer of the day, for the mount, a Capt. from Col. Burrel's Regt. For guard, 2 men.

Mount Independence, November 25th, Ad 1776.

Regimental orders: The aminition in Col. Mott's Regt., drawn from the publick stores, is all to be returned in, except 8 rounds of cartredges, to the quarter master of the Regt. & he to take aceount of yr same and return it in the publick stores, as the men of this Regt. are required to do No more duty but as is nesasary for to prepare for their march. They (are) required to bring all the public tools , vis: Peck exces, spades, shovels and exes, excepting one to each comp., nesasary for the march, to the care of the quorter master, that they be returned in the publick stores, and he take a recept for the same. To this the commanders of comps. to give attention to be proformed. The men are to wash up their cloathing as itt is not only condusive to their health but nesisary to Make a solgier like appearance that they be clean & neat. And the officers and men (are to) see that no damage (is) done to the huts—that not only from Princeble but a gainst genll. order by

WILLIAM WORTHINGTON,
Leut. Col. and commander of Sd Regt.

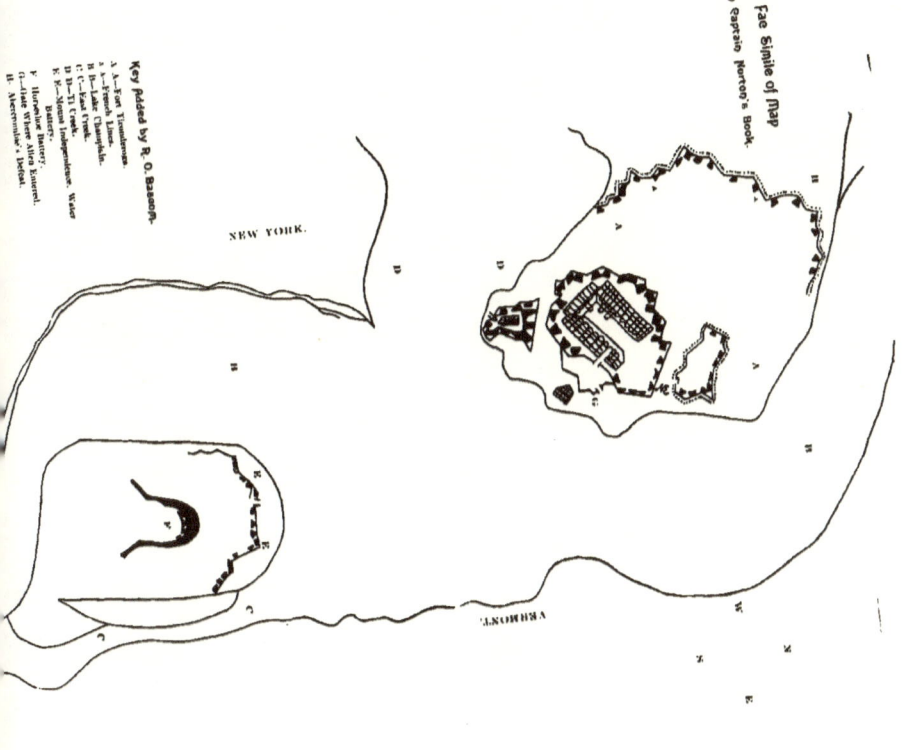

Fac Simile of Map
in Captain Norton's Book.

NEW YORK.

VERMONT.

Key Added by R. O. Bascom.

A—Fort Ticonderoga.
I—French Lines.
B—Lake Channlain.
C—Outlet Creek.
D—Lt. T. Creek.
E—Mount Independence Water
    Battery.
F—Horseshoe Battery.
G—Lake West Alien Removed.
H—Ancortnidoc; Defeat.